Other titles in the series:
The World's Greatest Computer Cartoons
The World's Greatest Dad Cartoons
The World's Greatest Golf Cartoons

Published simultaneously in 1993 by Exley Publications in Great Britain, and Exley Giftbooks in the USA.

Selection © Exley Publications Ltd.
ISBN 1-85015-440-6

Front cover illustration by Roland Fiddy.
Designed by Pinpoint Design.
Edited by Mark Bryant.
Printed and bound by Grafo, S.A. – Bilbao, Spain.

Exley Publications Ltd, 16 Chalk Hill, Watford, Herts WD1 4BN, United Kingdom.
Exley Giftbooks, 359 East Main Street, Suite 3D, Mount Kisco, NY 10549, USA.

THANK YOU

We would like to thank all the cartoonists who submitted entries for *The World's Greatest CAT CARTOONS*. They came in from many parts of the world - including Ireland, New Zealand, Germany, Canada, Holland, the United Kingdom and the USA.

Special thanks go to the cartoonists whose work appears in the final book. They include Enzo Apicella page 47; Les Barton pages 10, 12, 55, 60; Neil Bennett page 54; John Donegan page 26; Stidley Easel pages 17, 21, 23, 28, 29, 36, 39, 41, 42, 57; Roland Fiddy cover, title page and pages 14, 24, 43, 67, 70, 71; Noel Ford page 4; Gagan page 8; Toni Goffe pages 6, 16, 18, 31, 59, 65, 66, 75, 78; Gerard Hoffnung pages 50, 51; Tony Husband pages 5, 33, 34, 37, 46, 62, 64, 73; Cath Jackson page 48; Henry Martin page 7; David Myers pages 11, 32, 35, 38, 40, 45, 56, 69, 72, 76; Viv Quillin pages 9, 94; Bryan Reading page 44; George Sprod page 27; Bill Stott pages 20, 22, 25, 58, 61, 63, 68, 74, 79; Robert Thompson page 53; Matthew Van Fleet page 19; Steve Way page 52; Mike Williams pages 13, 15, 30, 77.

Every effort has been made to trace the copyright holders of cartoons in this book. However any error will gladly be corrected by the publisher for future printings.

THE WORLD'S GREATEST

CAT
CARTOONS

EDITED BY
Mark Bryant

EXLEY
MT. KISCO, NEW YORK • WATFORD, UK

"She spoils that cat."

"Can he call you back? — He's teaching the cat to drink milk."

TONI GOFFE

"You know what I like about you? You don't
talk, talk, talk, talk, talk, talk, talk!"

8

Spellbound

behind every gifted woman, there's often a rather talented cat
Quillin

"This looks like a good place to stay!"

"You spoil that cat."

"Oh, dear. I had a feeling the cat might contest."

13

"You spoil that cat."

15

*"I don't know what you're eating but the litter box
is filled with Little Friskies."*

"Normally I'd have to admit you're a pretty hum-drum
kind of guy. But with that can-opener in your hand, you're a giant."

Easel

"There's a furry thing in here eating cheese. I understand
that's your department."

"I suppose they think that's funny."

GLASS BOTTOMED BOAT

Easel

Easel

"Aww, did the wittle putty wutty kwime too high and did the wittle putty wutty give himself a natty fwight, or is the wittle putty wutty just a pea-brained smeg-head who can't tell his arse from his elbow?"

"Now I want a straight answer — _that_ didn't get there by itself."

"Don't give me that 'holier than thou' look, where's the canary?"

"Cat, where?... Bloody Hell, it must have eaten the parrot!"

"The cat got it.."

"He's the best mouser we've ever had."

"That cat must go..."

"You've got to hand it to him — that cat's a born trier..."

Easel

Easel

"Oh, no! Not Mrs Blenthorpe and her kitten again."

"I love hunting but I could never afford to go to Africa."

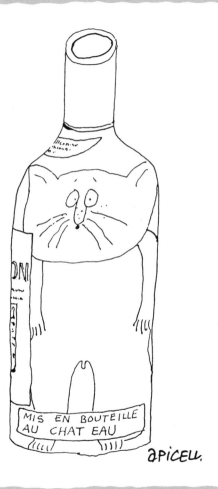

MIS EN BOUTEILLÉ
AU CHAT EAU

apicell.

47

JACKSON

53

"I don't think he's got the hang of the cat flap yet."

55

"They've always got on wonderfully together."

Easel

"You must tell me if he's being a nuisance..."

59

"I never throw rotten compost at your cat.
He's too bloody artful — He stands in front of the greenhouse!"

"What did the nasty man do to mama's little soldier?"

"What's the matter, cat got your tongue?"

"Oh come, come — does she look like a cat
who'd make a smell?"

"Aargh! I'll be glad when his scratching post's fixed."

"Don't be alarmed. It's just his way of saying
'please don't hurt me'."

"He's a trifle upset at your having deserted him for two weeks."

"Oh dear! I don't think he wants to stop with us."

"I'll wait until someone comes by before I go and have a drink.
I just love those cries of middle class outrage."

"Bless him — he has such an endearing honesty..."

"Don't <u>do</u> that!"

"That cat always knows when it's the Open."

"Either you come in right now or you're out all night!"

Books in "The World's Greatest" series
($4.99 £2.99 paperback)

The World's Greatest Cat Cartoons
The World's Greatest Computer Cartoons
The World's Greatest Dad Cartoons
The World's Greatest Golf Cartoons

Books in the "Victim's Guide" series
($4.99 £2.99 paperback)

Award winning cartoonist Roland Fiddy sees the funny side to life's phobias, nightmares and catastrophes.

The Victim's Guide to the Dentist
The Victim's Guide to the Doctor
The Victim's Guide to Middle Age

Books in the "Crazy World" series
($4.99 £2.99 paperback)

The Crazy World of Aerobics (Bill Stott)
The Crazy World of Cats (Bill Stott)
The Crazy World of Cricket (Bill Stott)
The Crazy World of Gardening (Bill Stott)
The Crazy World of Golf (Mike Scott)
The Crazy World of the Greens (Barry Knowles)
The Crazy World of The Handyman (Roland Fiddy)
The Crazy World of Hospitals (Bill Stott)
The Crazy World of Housework (Bill Stott)
The Crazy World of the Leaner Driver (Bill Stott)
The Crazy World of Love (Roland Fiddy)

The Crazy World of Marriage (Bill Stott)
The Crazy World of Rugby (Bill Stott)
The Crazy World of Sailing (Peter Rigby)
The Crazy World of Sex (David Pye)

Books in the "Fanatics" series
($4.99 £2.99 paperback)

The **Fanatic's Guides** are perfect presents for everyone with a hobby that has got out of hand. Eighty pages of hilarious black and white cartoons by Roland Fiddy

The Fanatic's Guide to the Bed
The Fanatic's Guide to Cats
The Fanatic's Guide to Computers
The Fanatic's Guide to Dads
The Fanatic's Guide to Diets
The Fanatic's Guide to Dogs
The Fanatic's Guide to Husbands
The Fanatic's Guide to Money
The Fanatic's Guide to Sex
The Fanatic's Guide to Skiing

Great Britain: Order these super books from your local bookseller or from Exley Publications Ltd, 16 Chalk Hill, Watford, Herts WD1 4BN. (Please send £1.30 to cover post and packaging on 1 book, £2.60 on 2 or more books.)